INVASION ALERT!

INVASION OF THE STINK BUGS

DEVON PATRICK

Enslow PUBLISHING

Please visit our website, www.enslow.com. For a free color catalog of all our high-quality books, call toll free 1-800-398-2504 or fax 1-877-980-4454

Published in 2027 by
Enslow Publishing
2544 Clinton Street
Buffalo, NY 14224

Portions of this work were originally authored by Michael Rajczak and published as *Animal Invaders: Destroying Native Habitats: Attack of the Stink Bugs*. All new material in this edition is authored by Devon Patrick.

Cataloging-in-Publication Data
Names: Patrick, Devon.
Title: Invasion of the stink bugs / Devon Patrick.
Description: Buffalo, NY : Enslow Publishing, 2027. | Series: Invasion alert! | Includes glossary and index.
Identifiers: ISBN 9781978548428 (pbk.) | ISBN 9781978548435 (library bound) | ISBN 9781978548442 (ebook)
Subjects: LCSH: Stinkbugs--Juvenile literature. | Introduced insects--Juvenile literature. | Agricultural pests--Juvenile literature.
Classification: LCC SB945.P47 D486 2027 | DDC 632.754--dc23

Printed in China

Photos Credits: Cover, p. 1 junrong/Shutterstock.com; cover, p. 1, 3, 4, 6, 8, 10, 12, 14, 16, 18, 20, 22, 23, 24 (dot pattern) Nurin Nabila A/Shutterstock.com; p. 4, 6, 8, 10, 12, 14, 16, 18, 20 (sidebar frame) HST6/Shutterstock.com; p. 5 Niney Azman/Shutterstock.com; p. 7 Steven Ellingson/Shutterstock.com; p. 7 Mizkit/Shutterstock.com; p. 8 Misaso/Shutterstock.com; p. 9 Body Stock/Shutterstock.com; p. 11 Vinicius R. Souza/Shutterstock.com; p. 13 M. Schauer/Shutterstock.com; p. 15 Desintegrator/Shutterstock.com; p. 17 Abitofeverything.jpg/Shutterstock.com; p. 19 Nordiah/Shutterstock.com; p. 20 woopics/Shutterstock.com; p. 21 Pk_camera/Shutterstock.com

CPSIA compliance information: Batch #QSENS27: For further information, contact Enslow Publishing, New York, New York, at 1-800-398-2504.

CONTENTS

Words in the glossary appear in **bold** type the first time they are used in the text.

WHAT'S THAT SMELL?

Stink bugs are small **insects**. They don't bite, so they are not usually dangerous to humans. But they sure can be annoying! Stink bugs got their name because they ... well ... stink! When crushed or threatened, stink bugs will release a bad smell. This is their way of defending themselves.

These bugs are native to East Asian countries like Japan, China, and Korea. But since the late 1990s, stink bugs have been spreading across the United States! They're damaging crops and sneaking into homes from coast to coast.

STAY ALERT

Thousands of ships bring **products** to the United States from East Asia each month. Stink bugs likely crawled onto those ships and traveled all the way from Asia to North America.

Stink bugs are only about the size of a dime, but these tiny critters can cause big problems!

MEET THE STINK BUG

Stink bugs have six legs, two antennae, straw-like mouthparts, and an exoskeleton. The exoskeleton is a hard outer covering somewhat like a shell. It can be brown, green, black, or gray. Their underside is white. Stink bugs are just under 1 inch (2.5 cm) long and have wings they use to fly.

Stink bugs love to eat fruits and vegetables! They cut them open with their mouthparts and suck out the juice. Don't worry, though—they don't bite people or animals.

STAY ALERT

All stink bugs have the same **shield**-shaped back. They're sometimes called shield bugs.

It can be fun to look at insects using a magnifying glass or **microscope**. A stink bug would be quite interesting to see up close!

STINKY BUGS

On the underside of all stink bugs is a pocket called a gland. This is where a smelly liquid is stored. When stink bugs feel scared, such as when a **predator** is near, they open the gland and give off a horrible smell. That stinky smell makes the predator go away.

Stink bugs also have a different smell they can let out to gather nearby stink bugs together. This smell is much less stinky to people—but it does mean that more stink bugs are coming!

STAY ALERT

Just like stink bugs, skunks use a smelly spray to scare attackers away. Skunks have to lift up their tail to spray the smell.

Don't step on a stink bug! Just one squished stink bug can make a whole room smell bad.

A GROWING PROBLEM

Stink bugs **reproduce** quickly. In the summer months, adult females lay about 25 eggs at a time every few days. Brown marmorated (MAHR-muh-ray-tuhd) stink bugs live for about six to eight months, and one female can lay up to 400 eggs in her lifetime. That's quite a lot of new stink bugs!

Since stink bugs are new to the United States, few bugs or animals hunt them regularly. As a result, their numbers keep growing and growing. Experts say this **invasive species** is a problem across the country.

STAY ALERT

Stink bugs were first seen in the United States in Pennsylvania. Today, they are found in almost every state.

Stink bug eggs are usually laid in clusters on the undersides of leaves.

ON THE FARM

There are many different species, or kinds, of stink bugs, but the brown marmorated stink bug gets a lot of attention. It feeds on more than 100 kinds of plants, such as those growing in farmers' fields. It damages crops so badly that many can't be sold or eaten.

Farmers can lose an entire crop to stink bugs. Selling fresh produce, which means fruits and vegetables, is how a farmer earns a living. With no produce to sell, the farmer loses a lot of money!

STAY ALERT

Other common stink bugs include the green stink bug and the brown stink bug.

Stink bugs' favorite foods are apples, peaches, tomatoes, corn, and soybeans. They also eat flowers, bushes, and trees.

A BIG PEST

Brown marmorated stink bugs don't like cold weather. So, they tend to come into people's homes in the fall to stay warm. They can hide in lots of tight spaces, like bookshelves, baseboards, and under your bed. They can be serious pests!

Finding a stink bug in your house may be frightening, but they won't harm your house or you. They don't bite, but they can bother some people. Be sure not to squish it, or you'll be in for a stinky surprise!

STAY ALERT

If you see a stink bug in your home, sweep it up and place it outside, or spray it with soapy water.

In the fall, stink bugs can often be found on the outside of buildings near doors or windows. Once inside your home, they can hide almost anywhere.

STAY OUT!

Stink bugs are spreading quickly across the United States. They may be winning for now, but there are a few ways people can fight back.

Since stink bugs like to come inside when the weather turns cold, sealing your home will keep stink bugs out. Windows and doors can be sealed with caulk, a thick goo used to fill cracks and holes. It's also important to fix holes in window screens. Stink bugs can even enter through the attic, chimney, or small cracks under the roof. These bugs are sneaky!

STAY ALERT

Adult stink bugs are good fliers, but young ones, called nymphs, can't fly yet. Adults fold their wings on top of their body when they land.

Stink bugs are drawn to bright lights. Changing the light bulbs outside your home to dimmer yellow lights can keep these bugs away.

PROTECTING CROPS

Stink bugs are a big problem for farmers and can **affect** the food supply. So, scientists and the government are working on the problem too. Dozens of scientists are studying the brown marmorated stink bug and learning how to fight it.

Gardeners can use a special spray made with clay to stop stink bugs from laying eggs on plants. Some farmers place plants that stink bugs like far away from their main crop. Others make stink bug traps with lures to capture the pests.

STAY ALERT

Stink bugs have become an established species in many areas of the country. This means there are many of them living and **breeding** in an area.

In the summer, stink bugs live in wooded areas, where they hide under leaves, shrubs, and logs. Cleaning up weeds and dead wood gets rid of places where they can make an easy home.

ON THE BRIGHT SIDE

Stink bugs are a stinky nuisance, but they aren't all bad! When a stink bug bites open tree bark, the tree releases sap. Wasps and ants feed on sap. Since both wasps and ants help to **pollinate** crops, it's good to help feed them. Nice work, stink bugs!

There's another way stink bugs could be good, but it's a little wacky: We can eat them! People eat insects in many places around the world. From crickets to bees, bugs can be delicious and **nutritious**!

STAY ALERT

When stink bugs spray, some people say it smells like strong herbs and spices, such as cilantro and coriander. Others say it smells like a skunk.

In some parts of the world, people eat stink bugs. Would you try one?

GLOSSARY

affect: to cause a change in someone or something

breeding: mating and giving birth to young

insect: a small, often winged, animal with six legs and three body parts

invasive species: one kind of living thing likely to spread and be harmful when placed in a new area

microscope: a scientific tool that uses lenses to enlarge tiny objects and living things

nutritious: containing things needed to grow and stay alive

pollinate: to take pollen from one flower, plant, or tree to another

predator: an animal that hunts other animals for food

product: something made or grown that is offered for sale

reproduce: to produce offspring

shield: a large plate of armor used in battle

FACT CHECK

1. A stink bug's smelly liquid is stored in its ________.
   a. gland b. shield c. antennae

2. Female stink bugs can lay up to __________ eggs in her lifetime.
   a. six to eight b. 25 c. 400

3. Stink bugs get inside people's homes in the ___________.
   a. spring b. summer c. fall

Answers: 1. a, 2. c, 3. c

ON THE INTERNET

Stink Bugs

www.pestworldforkids.org/pest-guide/stink-bugs/

Read a breakdown of stink bug information here.

Stink Bugs for Kids

www.youtube.com/watch?v=0l1WfNbt5ig&t=57s

Watch a short video about stink bugs from Learn Bright to learn all about these smelly insects!

Publisher's note to educators and parents: Our editors have carefully reviewed these websites to ensure that they are suitable for students. Many websites change frequently, however, and we cannot guarantee that a site's future contents will continue to meet our high standards of quality and educational value. Be advised that students should be closely supervised whenever they access the Internet.

INDEX